sl

slippers

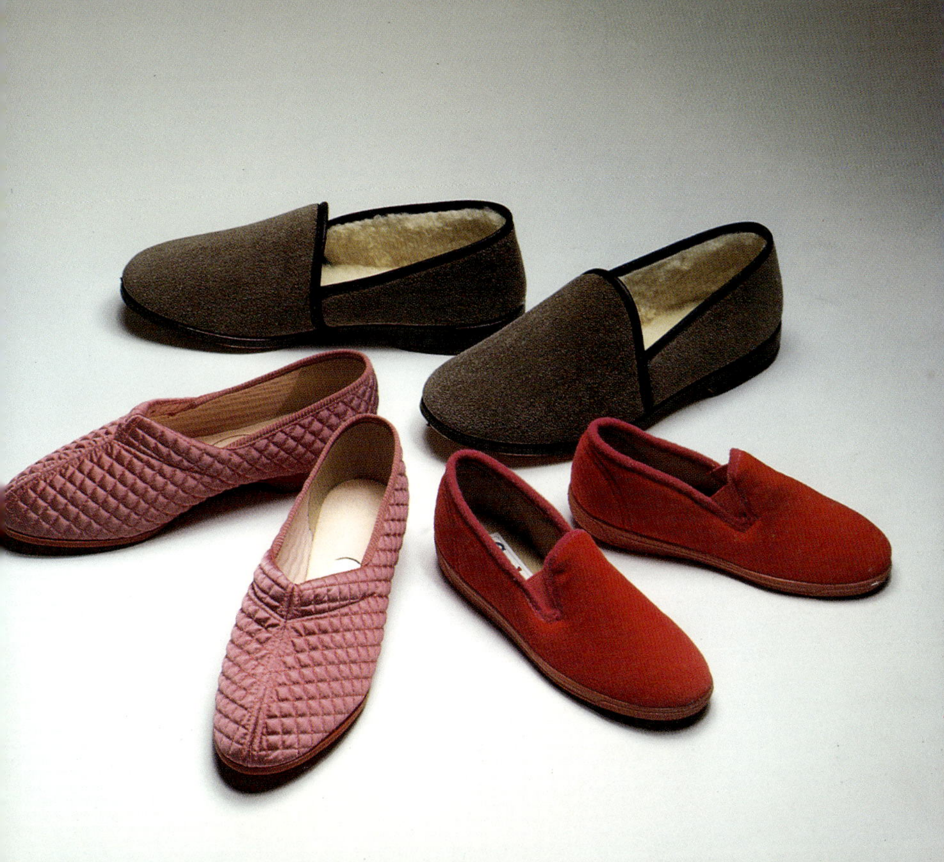

slide

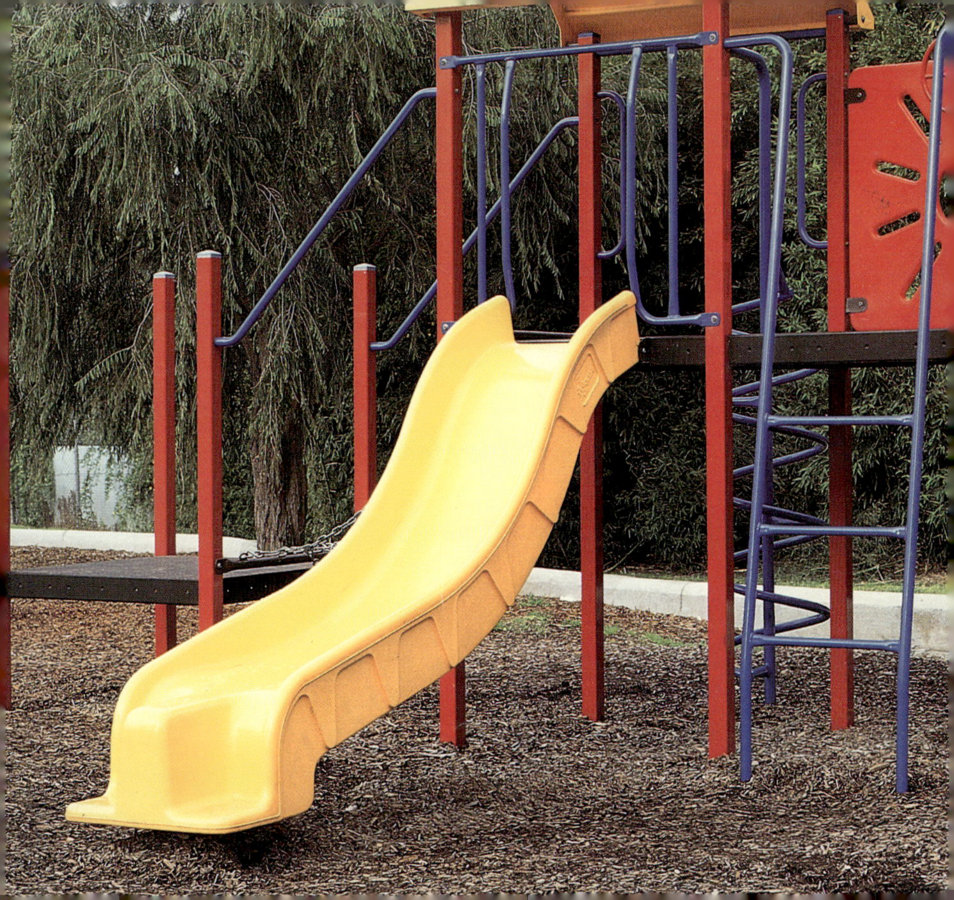

sleeve

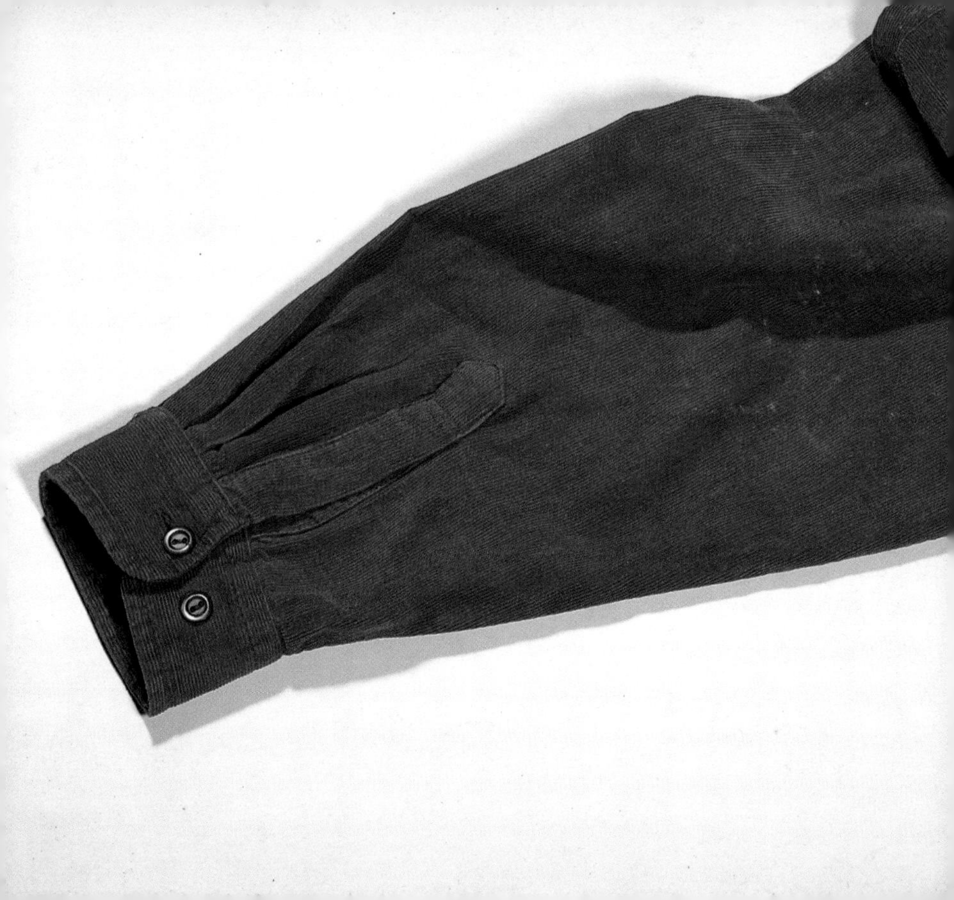

sling

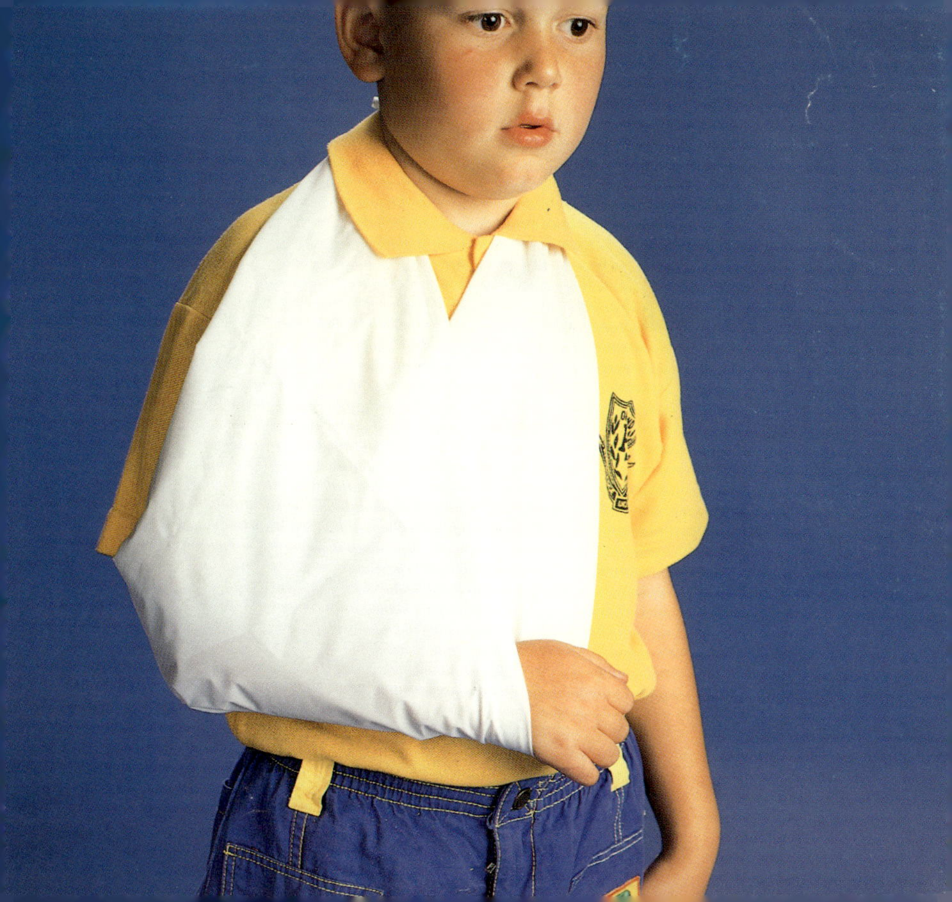

sled

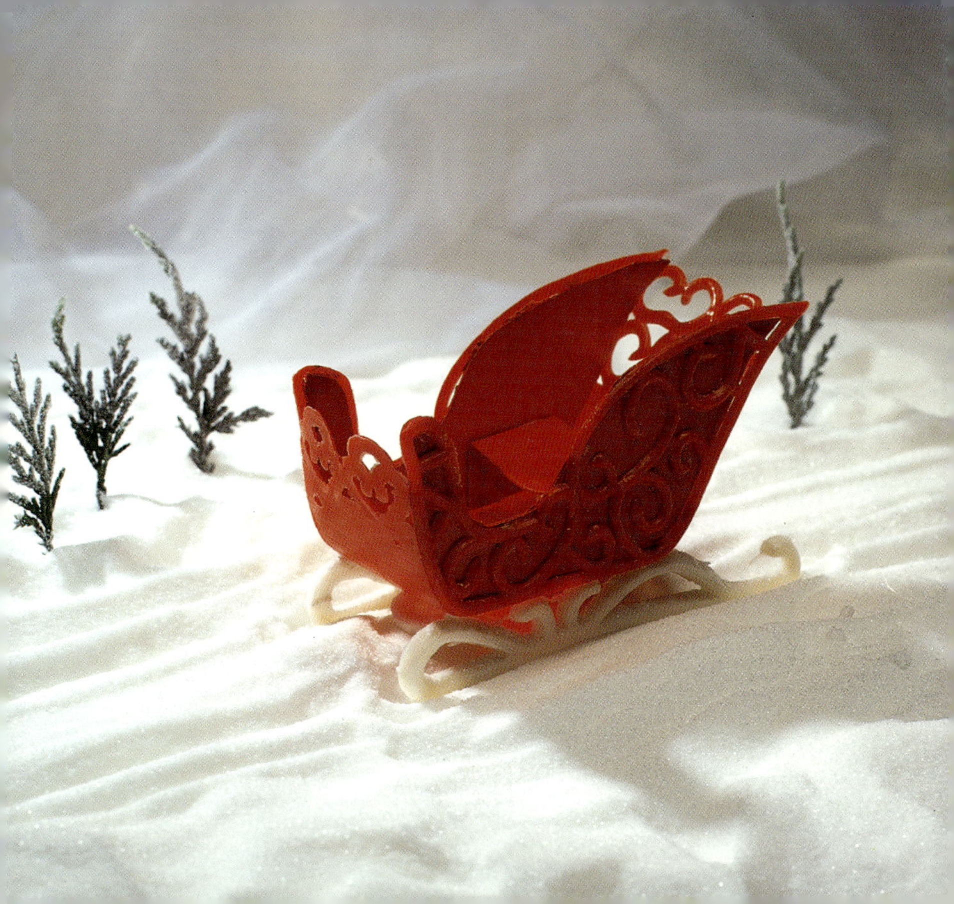

sl

slippers

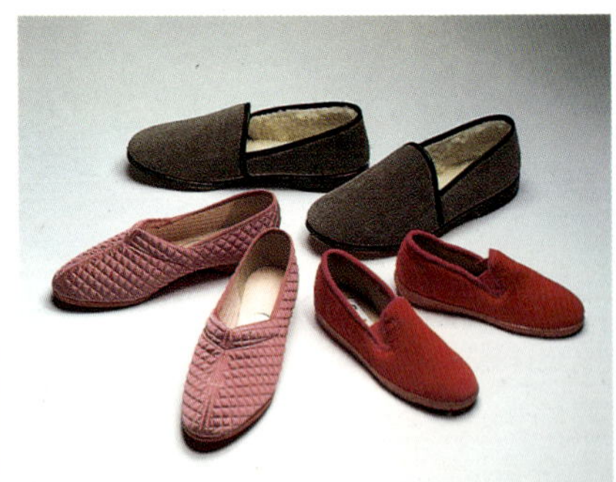